This Book Belongs to:

_____

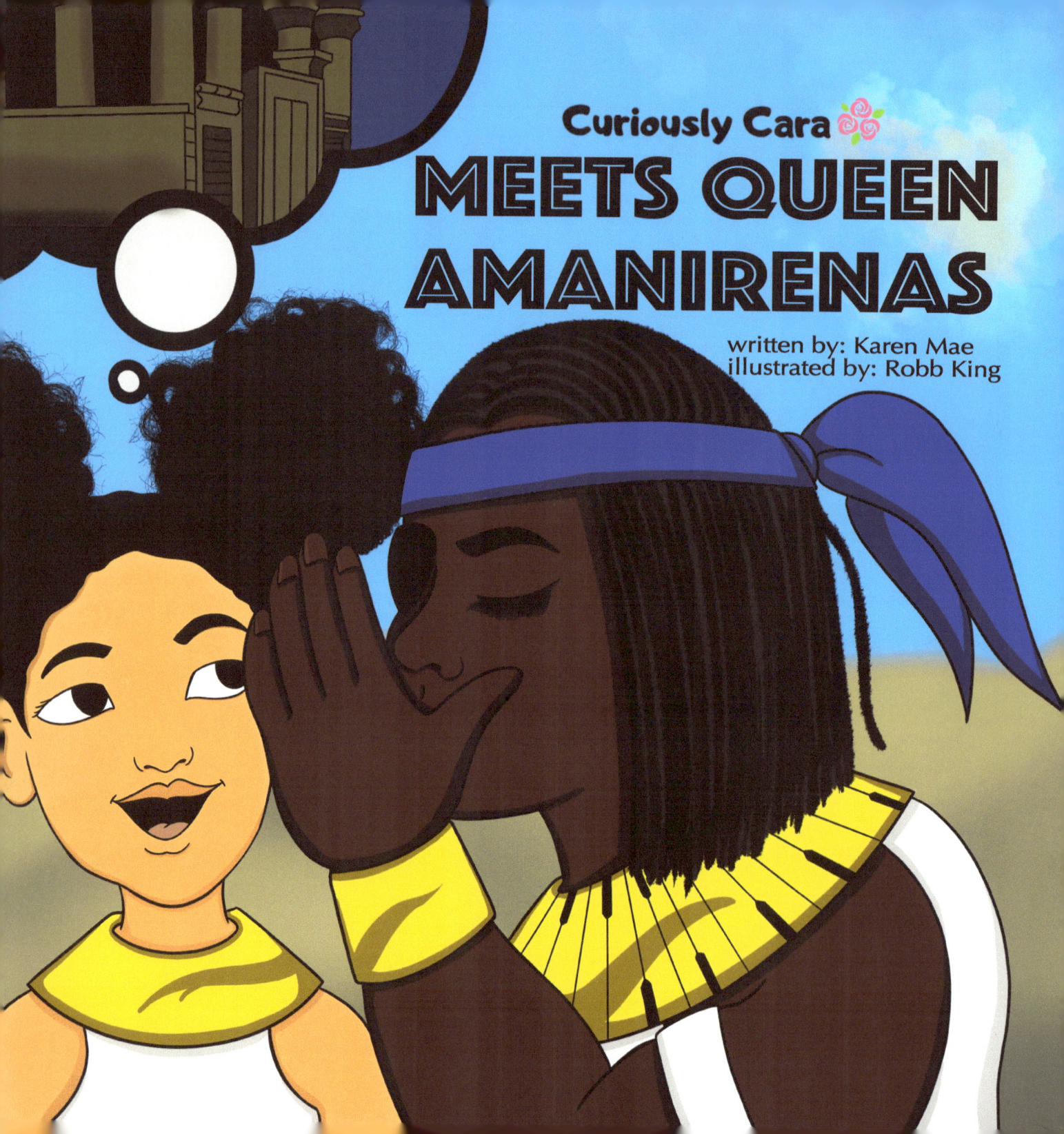

ALSO BY KAREN MAE
PART OF THE AFRICAN QUEENS SERIES

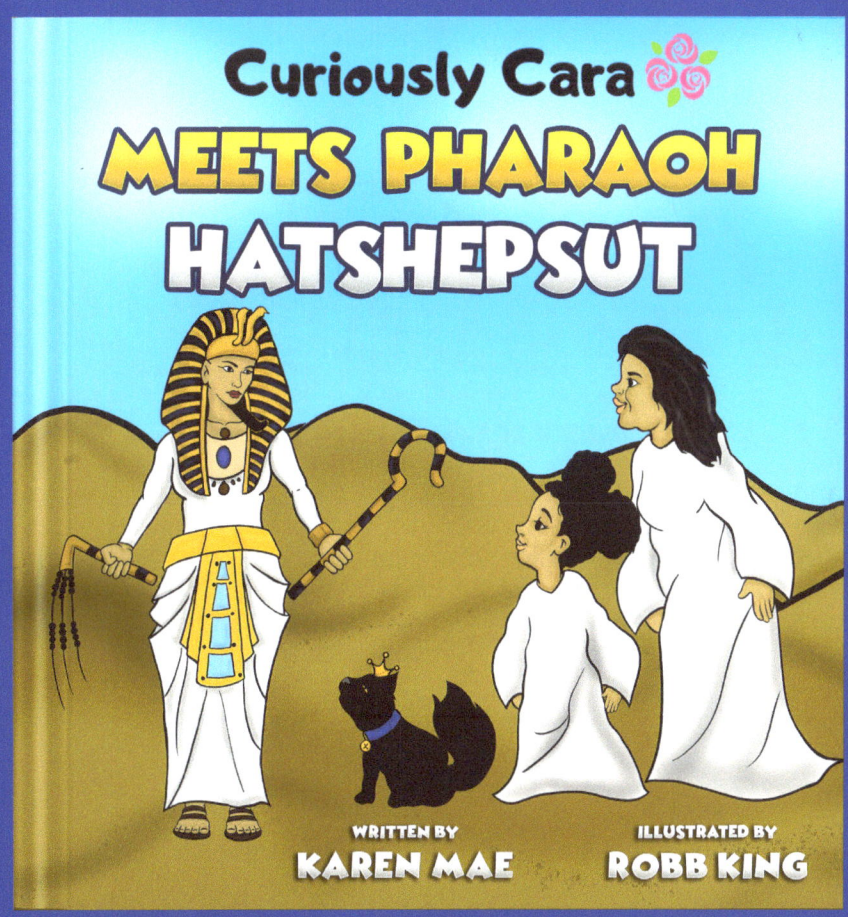

Tag Us #curiouslycara
Follow Us @curiously_cara

To all the little kings and queens, your brilliance matters.
~Karen

This is dedicated to my nephew, John. Keep dreaming, drawing, and creating. I love you.
~Robb

Copyright (c) 2023 by Karen Mae

Write and Vibe supports copyright. No part of this book may be used or reproduced in any matter whatsoever without written permission except in the case of brief quotations embodied in critical articles or reviews. Thank you for supporting creativity and copyright laws by not reproducing, scanning, or distributing any part of it in any form without permission. For permission requests, please write cori@writeandvibe.com.

www.writeandvibe.com

978-1-953430-16-8 (hardcover)

978-1-953430-14-4 (paperback)

978-1-953430-15-1 (digital)

DEFINITIONS

Archery: the sport or skill of shooting with bow and arrows

Bestow: giving someone a gift

Convoy: a group that travels together

Emperor: a person with great power and rank who usually rules a location

Kandake: a ruling queen that may also be known as a Queen Mother. Candace is the Latinized version of this term

Kushite: someone from The Kingdom of Kush

Prefect: a very important person that commands a group of people

Treaty: an agreement between countries

PRONUNCIATIONS

Amanirenas: uh-mah-nih-ree-nus

Caesar: see-zer

Gaius: guy-yus OR gay-yus

Kandake: kuhn-dok-kay

Kushite: kush-ite

Petronius: peh-tro-nee-us

Cara ran to her mommy with her big sister behind. "Amani says she's named after a queen!"

"I am!" huffed Amani.

Mommy smiled. "Amani is named after the very powerful, Queen Amanirenas."

"She fought in battles and everything." Amani kicked the air.

"Wow! What else did Queen Amanirenas do?" Cara asked.

Grandma walked outside with their cat, Daisy. "I think it's time for an adventure. Amani, you come too."

"Yay!" Cara and Amani jumped for joy and waved goodbye to Mommy.

Under the apple tree, they said their magic poem. "Dance to the left, circle to the right, ring Daisy's bell, and hold on tight."

Lastly, Cara yelled, "Three-two-one, let's have some fun!"

The magical funnel appeared and whisked them around and around.

When they opened their eyes, they were in a new land and Daisy wore her Adventure Crown that allowed her to talk, just like people!

"Are we in Egypt, again?" Cara asked when she saw they were in the desert.

Daisy responded, "We are a bit south of Egypt in ancient Nubia, where The Kushites lived in 22 BC. Today, it is the country, Sudan, but previously, it was known as The Kingdom of Kush."

"There are so many pyramids!" said Grandma.

Daisy looked around. "What you see are The Forgotten Pyramids and there are more than two hundred."

Grandma gasped, "They're marvelous."

Daisy continued, "The Kushites were miners, fantastic farmers, and builders. They were also warriors so skilled at archery that they were referred to as People of the Bow."

"Bow and arrows are cool!" Cara screeched.

Daisy shook sand from her hair. "One of the mighty warriors, and the one we're here to meet, was actually a Queen Mother, known as a Kandake." Her name is Queen Amanirenas and she needs your help."

Cara's mouth dropped open. "Why would she need our help?"

Daisy motioned Cara over. "You'll see. Be a dear and ring my bell, Queen Amanirenas has a story to tell."

When it disappeared, the ground shook and they saw a massive number of people holding swords, shields, and bow and arrows.

"Daisy, I think something went wrong with our poem," gasped Amani. "We didn't go anywhere and now we're surrounded by an army!"

A woman with an eye patch sat on top of an elephant, yelling down to the army.

"I think she's Queen Amanirenas," Cara pointed.

The Queen roared! "We have battled the Romans for five long years. To protect our families, we must win the war today!"

"Battle?" Cara shrieked.

Daisy explained, "After the Romans took over Egypt, they traveled to Kush and the fight began. In one of the battles, Queen Amanirenas lost an eye and she even chopped a head off of a statue!"

Queen Amanirenas yelled, "Emperor Caesar Augustus and Prefect Gaius Petronius want to take over our land and force us to pay them taxes, but we will not!"

When The Queen stopped talking, she noticed Cara and her family. "Come forward, young queen. What are you doing here?"

Cara was nervous to be near a mighty warrior. "I think we're here to help you end the war."

Queen Amanirenas hopped off her elephant. "You are too little to fight."

"I don't want to fight," replied Cara. "And I don't think anyone should fight, not even you. You should talk things over with Emperor Augustus, like adults."

"You believe that talking will end this war?" Queen Amanirenas asked.

Cara nodded yes.

The Queen thought for a moment. "Then we will try it. We must hurry!"

They rushed away on elephants with Queen Amanirenas leading the way. The archers and tens of thousands of soldiers marched behind.

When they arrived, Queen Amanirenas held up her fist for her convoy to stop.

Emperor Augustus and Prefect Petronius stood, waiting for them.

"And you should want the same for your people," Amani added.

Emperor Augustus squinted at them. "I'm listening."

"There is no reason to fight each other," started Cara.

Grandma giggled in the background and Amani said, "Good grief!"

Cara wagged her finger at Emperor Augustus. "Just like it's wrong to chop off statue heads, it's also wrong to take The Kushite's land. That's stealing."

The Emperor tapped his chin. "But their land has valuables that we need."

Queen Amanirenas thought for a moment. "You also have valuables that we could use. Perhaps, you would be willing to trade with us."

"We could do that," said The Emperor.

Cara smiled. "Great! And since there will be no more fighting, you will also need to remove your soldiers from The Kingdom of Kush."

"We will do so only if Queen Amanirenas also agrees to remove her soldiers from our land," Emperor Augustus bargained.

"I will call them home," said Queen Amanirenas.

Prefect Petronius whispered to The Emperor and The Emperor said, "We will help as long as you give back the head to my statue."

"It's a deal," said Queen Amanirenas.

Emperor Augustus and The Queen signed a treaty and the girls high-fived.

"Excellent job!" Grandma clapped.

"Thank you for your help today. As a parting gift, I bestow to each of you, golden bow and arrows."

"It has been a pleasure, Queen Amanirenas," Grandma said, "but I must get these young queens home."

Before they could say their magic poem, Cara yelled, "Wait! What happens to The Kushites now? Will the Romans leave them alone?"

Daisy answered, "The treaty allows them to continue living peacefully for hundreds of years with a long line of Kandakes."

Satisfied with the answer, they said their magic poem. "Much is now known, so it's time to go home."

Cara jingled Daisy's bell and instantly, the magical funnel appeared and transported them home.

Further reading (Books)

Commey, Pusch. **Seven Amazing African Queens and Dynasties.** Real African Books. 2018

Imhotep. **My African Icons: Great People in Black History.** Mr. Imhotep. 2020

Schwarz-Bart. **In Praise of Black Women 1: Ancient African Queens.** The University of Wisconsin Press. 2001

Further reading (Websites)

Statue. The British Museum. September 6, 2020. https://www.britishmuseum.org/collection/object/G_1911-0901-1

Mora, Kai. **The Nubian Queen Who Fought Back Caesar's Army.** History. March 23, 2022.

Magak, Adhiambo Edith. **The One-Eyed African Queen Who Defeated the Roman Empire.** Narratively. September 23, 2021

Further watching (YouTube)

Zeinab Badawi. **Kingdom of Kush - History OF Africa with Zeinab Badawi (Episode 4).** BBC News Africa. April 10, 2020. YouTube video 44:48

The Roman-Kushite War (27 BC - 22BC) | Total War Cinematic Documentary. Legendarian. May 9, 2021. YouTube video 7:19.

The African Queen Who Stood Against Rome. HomeTeam History, November 25, 2018. YouTube video, 4:11.

Geoff Emberling. **What happened to the lost Kingdom of Kush? - Geoff Emberling.** TED-Ed. October 7, 2021. YouTube video 4:34.

A Note About Queen Amanirenas

Queen Amanirenas was a top notch warrior, leader, and queen who fought off one of the most powerful armies at the time, The Roman Army. Although her story abruptly ends here, it continued on in real life. The treaty signed by The Romans and The Kushites was highly favorable to The Kushites, which allowed them to continue living on their own terms for hundreds of years.

A Note About Caesar Augustus

Caesar Augustus was a man of many names, including: Gaius Julius Caesar, Gaius Octavius, Julius Caesar Augustus, and others. In this book we chose to refer to him only as Caesar Augustus.

Hey Kids!

Cara and Amani helped Queen Amanirenas negotiate a treaty to stop the fighting. How would you have helped?

_____

_____

_____

_____

_____

_____

_____

_____

_____

About the Authors

Karen Mae grew up in Lawrenceburg, Indiana. As a book lover and avid reader, she always wanted to be a writer and to travel, but passed away before she could do so. Now, her daughter, Cori, authors the Curiously Cara series in Karen's name so symbolically, Karen can be a writer who travels with her grandchildren.

KAREN MAE

CORI

About Vibes: We are an independent publishing company that believes writers should only have to worry about writing. Meaning, you write your book, we'll do the rest.

To learn more about us, our authors, and their books, please visit us at

Writeandvibe.com | Fb & IG @writeandvibe